FOOTBALL'S BIGGEST RIVALRIES

by Matt Doeden

CAPSTONE PRESS
a capstone imprint

Published by Capstone Press, an imprint of Capstone
1710 Roe Crest Drive, North Mankato, Minnesota 56003
capstonepub.com

Library of Congress Cataloging-in-Publication Data
Names: Doeden, Matt, author.
Title: Football's biggest rivalries / by Matt Doeden.
Description: North Mankato, Minnesota : Capstone Press, [2024] | Series: Sports Illustrated kids. Great sports rivalries | Includes bibliographical references and index. | Audience: Ages 8 to 11 | Audience: Grades 4-6 | Summary: "Competition can be fierce on the football field. From NFL matchups to college clashes, teams and players give their all, and passionate fans support them every step of the way. Learn the history behind some of football's biggest rivalries and decide who comes out on top."—Provided by publisher.
Identifiers: LCCN 2022050196 (print) | LCCN 2022050197 (ebook) | ISBN 9781669049104 (hardcover) | ISBN 9781669049050 (paperback) | ISBN 9781669049067 (pdf) | ISBN 9781669049081 (kindle edition) | ISBN 9781669049098 (epub)
Subjects: LCSH: Football teams—Juvenile literature. | Sports rivalries—Juvenile literature.
Classification: LCC GV950.7 .D6284 2024 (print) | LCC GV950.7 (ebook) | DDC 796.332—dc23/eng/20221027
LC record available at https://lccn.loc.gov/2022050196
LC ebook record available at https://lccn.loc.gov/2022050197

Editorial Credits
Editor: Alison Deering; Designer: Elyse White; Media Researcher: Rebekah Hubstenberger; Production Specialist: Whitney Schaefer

Image Credits
Associated Press: AP Photo/File, 12, Charles Krupa, 28, Harry Harris, 10, Jerry Hoefer, 16; Getty Images: Bettmann, 13, Gregory Shamus, 8, iStock/David Madison, 5, Jamie Squire, 21, Jed Jacobsohn, 18, Jeff Haynes/Sports Illustrated, 29, Kevin C. Cox, 6, 7, Michael Zagaris, 24, Mike Mulholland, 9, Peter Aiken, 20, Quinn Harris, 15, Richard Rodriguez, 17; Shutterstock: Andrew Angelov, 4, Brian Goff, design element (football icon), Jansx Customs, design element (lines), vectortatu, design element (vs.); Sports Illustrated: Al Tielemans, 11, 26, Damian Strohmeyer, 27, Erick W. Rasco, cover (middle right), Hy Peskin, 22, John Biever, cover (middle left), 14

All internet sites appearing in back matter were available and accurate when this book was sent to press.

TABLE OF CONTENTS

Words in **bold** are in the glossary.

Gridiron Grudges

The quarterback barks out signals. Defensive players crowd the **line of scrimmage**. The crowd roars. Pads crash together as the ball is snapped.

Football is always intense, but the **stakes** are even higher in rivalry games. What makes a rivalry great? Turn the page to find out and learn about some of football's greatest rivalries.

Chapter 1

College Rivals

College sports are filled with passion. Coaches, players, and fans put their hearts into the game. That emotion fuels rivalries that can last decades.

Auburn University vs. University of Alabama

These **conference** rivals battle for bragging rights in the state of Alabama. Their yearly game is so big that it has its own nickname—the Iron Bowl. The first game took place in 1893. Auburn won 32–22.

Since then, the Auburn Tigers and the Alabama Crimson Tide have become two of the most successful football programs in college history. Fans root *against* their rival almost as much as they root for their own team.

Chris Davis races to score the winning touchdown for the Auburn Tigers.

Auburn fans swarm the field after defeating the Crimson Tide.

These teams have had some epic matchups. In 2013, Auburn returned a missed Alabama field goal for a touchdown. The Tigers won as time expired. In 2021, Alabama came back late to tie the game 10–10. The teams played four overtime periods before Alabama finally won 24–22.

Stats

Total matchups: 86		
Alabama: 48	Auburn: 37	tie: 1
Total points		
Alabama: 1,852	Auburn: 1,446	
Highest scoring game (2014)		
Alabama: 55	Auburn: 44	
Lowest scoring game (1960)		
Alabama: 3	Auburn: 0	

Ohio State University vs. University of Michigan

The Michigan Wolverines and Ohio State Buckeyes first met in 1897. Both teams went on to join the Big Ten Conference and have fought for control ever since.

In 1950, the teams battled in a blizzard. The game, called the Snow Bowl or Blizzard Bowl, featured 45 punts! Michigan won the game 9–3.

In 2006, the Buckeyes hosted the Wolverines in the final game of the regular season. Both teams were 11–0. The "Game of the Century" lived up to the **hype**. Ohio State's Brian Robiskie scored a touchdown with five minutes left. He sealed it for the Buckeyes. They won 42–39.

The Buckeyes celebrated after taking the lead during a 2006 matchup.

In 2021, Michigan shocked Ohio State. Wolverines running back Hassan Haskins scored five touchdowns. Michigan won the game 42–27. They won again in 2022, beating Ohio State 45–23 and proving the rivalry is alive and well.

Wolverines fans raced to the field following their team's 2021 victory over Ohio State.

Stats

All-time series	
Michigan leads, 60–51–6	

Big Ten championships	
Michigan: 43	Ohio State: 39

National championships	
Michigan: 11	Ohio State: 8

Army vs. Navy

Army vs. Navy is a rivalry that goes beyond football. As **military academies**, the schools don't have access to as many players as top colleges. But there's something about Army vs. Navy that football fans can't resist.

The competition dates back to 1890. The height of the rivalry came in 1944 and 1945. The two teams met while ranked number one and two in the nation.

Army won in 1944. Both teams were undefeated going into the 1945 contest. The Army Black Knights rolled over the Navy Midshipmen 32–13. They went on to win the national title.

Army cadets were ready to cheer on their team ahead of the 1954 rivalry game.

The rivals face off at the line of scrimmage.

The rivalry lives on today. For Army, it's "Beat Navy!" For Navy, it's "Beat Army!" The chants go beyond football, extending to a friendly rivalry between the two military services.

Fun Fact

10 sitting United States presidents have attended an Army-Navy football matchup. The first was Theodore Roosevelt in 1901.

Chapter 2

Epic NFL Rivalries

Sometimes, two National Football League (NFL) teams just see too much of each other. Bad blood between players and fans creates rivalries that take games to a new level.

Chicago Bears vs. Green Bay Packers

Bears vs. Packers is the NFL's oldest rivalry. The teams have been butting heads for more than 100 years. In 1921, the Chicago Staleys beat the Packers 20–0 in their first game. Two years later, they won again, this time as the Chicago Bears.

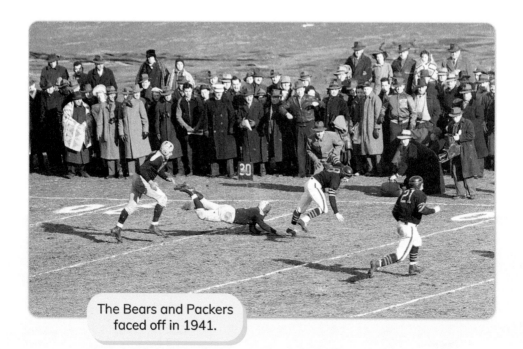

The Bears and Packers faced off in 1941.

Chicago used a hard-hitting style to **dominate** much of the early 1900s. The teams tied for the Western Division crown in 1941, forcing a playoff. Chicago crushed Green Bay 33–14.

In 1959, Vince Lombardi became head coach of the Packers. Under him, Green Bay took control of the rivalry. They owned the 1960s, winning five league championships, including two Super Bowls.

Led by Lombardi (center), the Packers won the first Super Bowl in 1967.

Over the next several decades, both teams had their ups and downs. They met in the National Football Conference (NFC) Championship after the 2010 season. The Bears came up short. The Packers won 21–14 and went on to win the Super Bowl.

Green Bay Packers Diyral Briggs proudly holds a newspaper celebrating his team's Super Bowl win.

A Green Bay supporter echoes Aaron Rodgers's taunt to Bears fans.

The rivalry got extra heated in 2021. In October, the Packers traveled to Chicago. They defeated the Bears 24–14. The win moved Green Bay quarterback Aaron Rodgers to 22–5 all-time against Chicago.

Rodgers didn't let it go unnoticed. He taunted Chicago fans, telling them, "I own you." The comments didn't go over well with Bears fans. This is one rivalry that could be going strong for another 100 years.

Dallas Cowboys vs. Washington Commanders

The rivalry between Dallas and Washington started before they ever played a game. In 1960, the Cowboys entered the NFL as an **expansion team**. They signed longtime Washington quarterback Eddie LeBaron. Washington fans were furious.

A Cowboys player holds the funeral wreath his team received as he marches to the Washington locker room.

The Cowboys spent the 1970s building a **dynasty**. In 1979, the teams met in the final game of the season. The winner would be the division champ. Someone sent the Cowboys a funeral wreath. It was their way of saying the dynasty was dead.

It looked like they were right. Washington led by 13 late in the game. But Dallas quarterback Roger Staubach led an amazing comeback. He threw the game-winning touchdown pass with less than a minute left.

After the game, one of the Cowboys players rushed into the Washington locker room. He threw the wreath at the Washington players.

The Cowboys have dominated this rivalry in recent decades. From 1997 to 2002, they came out on top in 10 straight matchups against the Commanders.

The Cowboys also lead in Super Bowl titles. To date, they have five. The Commanders have won three Super Bowls.

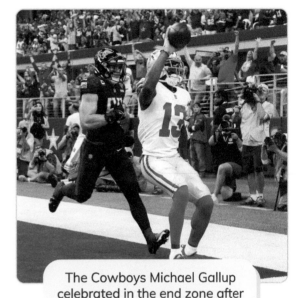

The Cowboys Michael Gallup celebrated in the end zone after scoring a touchdown against the rival Commanders in 2022.

Stats

All-time series		
Dallas: 75	Commanders: 45	tie: 2

All-time score (regular season)	
Dallas: 2,889	Commanders: 2,375

Division titles	
Dallas: 24	Washington: 15

Super Bowl titles	
Dallas: 5	Washington: 3

Baltimore Ravens vs. Cleveland Browns

In 1995, the Browns shocked fans. After more than 50 years in Cleveland, the team moved to Baltimore. They became the Ravens. Cleveland fans were left without a team.

The NFL acted quickly. It declared the Ravens were a new team. The Browns would return in 1999—officially as the same **franchise**. To spice things up, the two teams would play in the same division.

Browns fans were not happy to learn their team would be moving to Baltimore.

Browns fans hated the Ravens with a passion. Their anger oozed out every time the teams met. But Baltimore was a much stronger team. The Ravens dominated the rivalry. And they did it with players who had once been Browns.

Baltimore won the Super Bowl in 2001 and again in 2013. Meanwhile, Cleveland struggled as one of the league's worst teams.

The rivalry has been one-sided on the field. But Cleveland fans have not forgiven Baltimore for taking their team.

Stats

All-time record
Baltimore leads: 34–12

Total points
Baltimore leads: 1,107–735

Super Bowl titles

| Baltimore: 2 | Cleveland: 0 |

Kansas City Chiefs vs. Las Vegas Raiders

The Raiders have spent time in Oakland, Los Angeles, and Las Vegas. But one thing has remained the same. Their rivalry with the Kansas City Chiefs is as hot as any in the NFL.

The rivalry started when both teams were part of the American Football League (AFL). It continued when the AFL and NFL merged in 1970. Bad blood spilled over in the first NFL matchup between the teams. The benches cleared in a **brawl** between players.

Matchups between the Chiefs and Raiders often get heated.

Chiefs quarterback Patrick Mahomes (center) celebrates with his teammates following their Super Bowl LIV win.

The Raiders were one of the NFL's best teams in the 1970s and 1980s. Meanwhile, the Chiefs struggled. But things changed in 2017. Kansas City drafted quarterback Patrick Mahomes. Two seasons later, the Chiefs won the Super Bowl and took control of the rivalry.

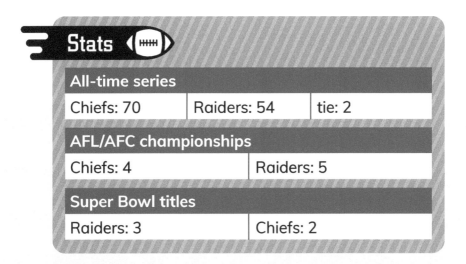

Stats

All-time series		
Chiefs: 70	Raiders: 54	tie: 2

AFL/AFC championships	
Chiefs: 4	Raiders: 5

Super Bowl titles	
Raiders: 3	Chiefs: 2

Chapter 3

It's Personal

Sometimes, rivalries are less about a team and more about two players. Friendly rivalries give fans the chance to argue who's the best.

Bobby Layne vs. Otto Graham

One of the NFL's first great quarterback rivalries started in the 1950s. Otto Graham was the league's biggest star. Starting in 1946, he led the Cleveland Browns to 10 straight NFL Championship games. But in 1952, the Detroit Lions were ready to take their shot at the Browns.

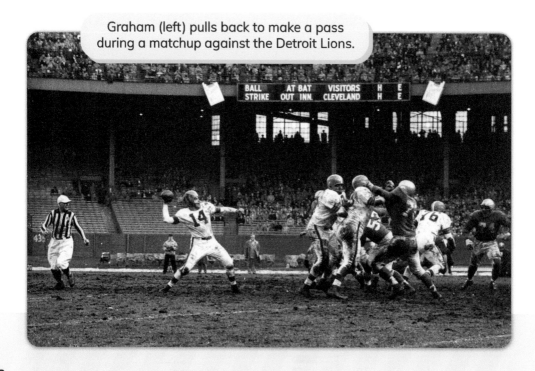

Graham (left) pulls back to make a pass during a matchup against the Detroit Lions.

The teams met in the 1952 NFL Championship. Most expected Graham to lead the Browns to victory. But Lions quarterback Bobby Layne had other ideas. The Lions won 17–7.

The teams met again in the 1953 NFL Championship. The Browns had the lead with four minutes left. But Layne fired a late touchdown pass to win 17–16.

Detroit went for three in a row in 1954. But this time, Graham shined. The Browns destroyed the Lions 56–10.

Stats

	Graham	Layne
Games played	126	175
Passing yards	23,584	26,768
Passing touchdowns	174	196
Interceptions	135	243
NFL Championships	3	3
NFL Most Valuable Player (MVP) awards	3	0

Joe Montana vs. Steve Young

Quarterback Joe Montana led the San Francisco 49ers in the 1980s. He was **accurate** and cool under pressure. But by the late 1980s, he had competition—backup quarterback Steve Young.

The **debate** raged in San Francisco and around the league. Montana struggled to stay healthy. Young looked like a star every chance he got. The 49ers gave Young some time but mostly stuck with Montana.

In 1991, Montana suffered an elbow injury. Young finally took over. He went on to win two league MVPs and a Super Bowl.

Montana (left) watches as Young talks to the 49ers head coach.

Montana moved on to the Kansas City Chiefs. In 1994, the two met on the field for the only time in their careers. Montana got revenge on his old team. He threw two touchdown passes. The Chiefs beat the 49ers 24–17.

Stats

	Montana	Young
Games played	192	169
Passing yards	40,551	33,124
Passing touchdowns	273	232
Interceptions	139	107
Super Bowl titles	4	3

Fun Fact

Montana and Young aren't the only example of two star quarterbacks sharing a team. In 2005, the Packers drafted Aaron Rodgers, even though they had future Hall-of-Famer Brett Favre on the team. Rodgers waited his turn, finally taking over for Favre in 2008. Favre ended up with the rival Minnesota Vikings. In 2010, he led the Vikings to the NFC Championship Game.

Peyton Manning vs. Tom Brady

In the 2000s, Indianapolis Colts vs. New England Patriots was must-watch football. Both teams were among the best in the American Football Conference (AFC). But for most fans, it was really about two quarterbacks. The Colts had Peyton Manning. The Patriots had Tom Brady.

The two players took very different routes to the NFL. Manning was the son of a star quarterback. He was a number-one draft pick. He had a cannon for an arm and accuracy to go with it.

Manning points the way on the field.

Brady was largely overlooked coming out of college. He wasn't picked until the sixth round. But once he got his chance, he did nothing but win.

Brady charges down the field during a game against the Colts.

The two superstars met after the 2003 season in the AFC Championship. Brady and the Patriots outmatched Manning and the Colts. The Patriots won 24–14.

Three years later, it was a rematch. Brady and the Patriots were in the lead early. But Manning led a thrilling comeback. The Colts scored the winning touchdown with a minute left.

The two star quarterbacks shared a hug after their January 2004 AFC matchup.

Manning moved to the Denver Broncos in 2012. After the 2015 season, the pair met for the final time in the AFC Championship. Brady led New England to a touchdown with 12 seconds left. But the Broncos held on to win 20–18. Denver went on to win the Super Bowl, and Manning **retired** a champion.

Manning headed back to the field to celebrate after the Colts beat the Patriots in the 2016 AFC Championship.

Brady played on. In 2020, he moved to the Tampa Bay Buccaneers. He led the team to its second Super Bowl win. It was Brady's tenth Super Bowl and seventh win. In 2023, Brady announced his official retirement after 23 seasons in the NFL.

Stats

Regular season wins (head-to-head)	
Brady: 9	Manning: 3

Postseason wins (head-to-head)	
Manning: 3	Brady: 2

Super Bowl titles	
Brady: 7	Manning: 2

NFL MVP awards	
Manning: 5	Brady: 3

Glossary

accurate (AK-yuh-ruht)—able to do something precisely and without error

brawl (BRAWL)—a rough fight

conference (KAHN-fuhr-uhns)—an association of athletic teams

debate (di-BATE)—a discussion between two sides with different ways of thinking on a subject; each side tries to convince people that it is right

dominate (DAH-muh-nayt)—to rule; in sports, a team or person dominates if they win much more than anyone else

dynasty (DYE-nuh-stee)—a team that wins multiple championships over a period of several years

expansion team (ik-SPAN-shuhn TEEM)—a new team in a league, made largely of players from existing teams

franchise (FRAN-chize)—a sports organization or team

hype (HAHYP)—excitement built up about an event

line of scrimmage (LINE UHV SKRIM-ij)—an imaginary line running across the width of a football field; each play beings at the line of scrimmage

military academy (MIL-i-ter-ee uh-KAD-uh-mee)—a school where military officers are trained

retire (ri-TAHYUHR)—to end one's career

stakes (STAYKS)—the prize in a contest

Read More

Bowen, Fred. *Gridiron: Stories from 100 Years of the National Football League.* New York: Margaret K. McElderry Books, 2020.

Cooper, Robert. *College Football.* Minneapolis: Pop!, 2020.

Lowe, Alexander. *G.O.A.T. Football Quarterbacks.* Minneapolis: Lerner Publications, 2023.

Internet Sites

National Football League
www.nfl.com

Pro Football Hall of Fame
www.profootballhof.com/

Sports Illustrated Kids: Football
www.sikids.com/football

Index

About the Author

Matt Doeden is a freelance author and editor from Minnesota. He has written numerous children's books on sports, music, current events, the military, extreme survival, and much more. His books *Basketball Shoes, Shorts, and Style; Dragons;* and *Could You Be a Monster Wave Surfer?* (all by Capstone Press) are Junior Library Guild selections. Doeden began his career as a sportswriter before turning to publishing. He lives in Minnesota with his wife and two children.

photo credit: Tracy Caffery